THE FURTHER ADVENTURES OF PETE SUSSMAN

THE FURTHER ADVENTURES
OF PETE SUSSMAN

New and Selected Poems

by Herb Guggenheim

iUniverse, Inc.
New York   Bloomington

The Further Adventures of Pete Sussman

New and Selected Poems

Copyright © 2008 by Herbert S. Guggenheim

All rights reserved. No part of this book may be used or reproduced by any means, graphic, electronic, or mechanical, including photocopying, recording, taping or by any information storage retrieval system without the written permission of the publisher except in the case of brief quotations embodied in critical articles and reviews.

iUniverse books may be ordered through booksellers or by contacting:

iUniverse
1663 Liberty Drive
Bloomington, IN 47403
www.iuniverse.com
1-800-Authors (1-800-288-4677)

Different versions of some of these poems have appeared in the *Beloit Poetry Journal, Dialogue,* the *GW Review, Phoebe,* and the *Washington Review.*

A version of "Pete Sussman Answers a Challenge from the Countess Lisa to Write a Sonnet in Less Than 24 Hours" appeared in the anthology *Cabin Fever: Poets at Joaquin Miller's Cabin, 1984-2001.* (Washington, DC: The Word Works, 2003).

Different versions of ten of these poems were published in the chapbook *Pomes, Buck Each: The First Pete Sussman Cycle.* by Herbert S. Guggenheim (Washington, DC: Ecclesiastes, 1994).

The poem "Pete Sussman Translates a Poem by Hugo von Hofmannsthal" is based upon "Wir gingen eine Weg..." ("We Were Walking Down a Road...") by Hugo von Hofmannsthal but is not an actual translation of that poem.

Because of the dynamic nature of the Internet, any Web addresses or links contained in this book may have changed since publication and may no longer be valid. The views expressed in this work are solely those of the author and do not necessarily reflect the views of the publisher, and the publisher hereby disclaims any responsibility for them.

ISBN: 978-1-4401-0485-5 (pbk)
ISBN: 978-1-4401-0486-2 (ebk)

Library of Congress Control Number: 2008940041
Printed in the United States of America

iUniverse rev. date: 12/22/08

Acknowledgments

The author wishes to express his appreciation to the core members of the Little Falls Writing Group: Paul T. Hopper, Luther Jett, Robin Pachtman, Jan Starkey, and Doug Wilkinson for their help and support.

The author wishes to thank his wife Leslie Carroll.

For Leslie

Table of Contents

1

What I Remember	3
Futurama II	4
Pete Sussman Tells His Son about the Fair	8
Pete Sussman Opens a Window	9
A Phone Call in the Dark	11
Among the Waves	13

2

Pete Sussman Answers a Challenge from the Countess Lisa to Write a Sonnet in Less Than 24 Hours	17
Pete Sussman Wonders Whether He Should Write a Poem about His Zoology Teacher's Feet	18
Pete Sussman Observes a Man Eating out of the Garbage	20
Pete Sussman Leaves on a Jet Plane	23
Without Forewarning, Sussman Quits His Job	26
Pete Sussman Translates a Poem by Hugo von Hofmannsthal	28
Pete Sussman Tries to Be Intentionally Clever, or "The *Fuck* Poem"	30
Pete Sussman Receives Some Advice From His Reflection	31
After a Long Absence, the Countess Lisa Returns to Pose a Startling New Set of Interrogatories	32
Pete Sussman—After the Storm Birds	33

3

Pete Sussman Returns to the Musée des Beaux Arts	37
Pete Sussman Dozes Off While Watching a Rerun of an Old *Gilligan's Island* Episode	38
What Will Be Remembered	40
The Death Poem	42
The Death Poem II	46

Pete Sussman Writes a Poem about Life   50
Pete Sussman Considers the Act of Remembering   53
The Problems of Philosophy   56
The Chinese Room   58

1

What I Remember

It's hot and humid. We are all alone
out here, in back, to garden for an hour.
Somewhere, far off, I hear a mower's drone
and catch the fragrance of a distant flower.

Too bad our marigolds don't smell as sweet.
I get down on my hands and knees to press
my nose into the flowers at your feet.
Then, looking up, I see your swirling dress.

Did I think things would always be like this?—
a yard, a house, some grass, a place to play—
a summer afternoon, a mother's kiss—
or did I know it all would melt away?

Before you knelt to plant those marigolds,
I wound myself into your dress's folds.

Futurama II

Now technology has found a way to penetrate and control the wild profusion of this wonder world. A jungle road is built in one continuous operation. First, a searing ray of light–a laser beam—cuts through the trees. Then a giant machine, a factory on wheels, grinds up the stumps and jungle growth, sets the firm foundations, forms the surface slabs, sets them in place and the roadway bed is paved. These forest highways now are bringing to the innermost depths of the tropic world the goods and materials of progress and prosperity creating productive communities that can enter profitably the markets of the world and offering to us all enchanting tours through the storybook forests of tropic lands.

—from the Futurama II Ride Narrative
General Motors Pavilion
New York World's Fair
1964–'65

I keep having this dream.

After the World's Fair ended in 1965,
they demolished the buildings,
tore everything down
except the Unisphere—
that giant globe you sometimes see in movies.

The fair grounds (I've been told) are now a park—
Flushing Meadows it's called.
But, in my dream, the General Motors Pavilion is still there
and—*miraculously*—they've opened it up again.

Well—sort of.

In '64 we stood on line then sat in moving chairs that passed
    through—*well*—
environments—
sweeping dioramas of the future—

a moon base,
a space station,
a dome in the Antarctic,
a rain forest.

And, in my dream,
a group of elderly preservationists
wants to—*somehow*—

revive the fair
maybe rebuild it
or build a new one.
I'm not really sure.

And, like I said,
they've actually managed to open this building
and they've got *Futurama II* up and running again.
You can even ride it if you want to.

Only the dioramas were ripped out long ago and the building's in
    ruins—
plywood in its vast empty lobby
and places where yellowed sunlight shines in through plaster
where the outside of the building has crumbled and fallen away.

There isn't a line, of course,
because not many people care about this sort of thing.
(Most people come to Flushing Meadows to walk their dogs or play
    Frisbee.)
But, if you're a history nut, you can go.

The area just before the ride is undecorated
and kind of looks like it's under construction.
The ride apparatus is noisy from decades of disuse.
You can hear the gears and belts grinding laboriously as you get closer.
And you can smell the odor of hot hydraulic fluid.

You board this slow moving ride like you would the ones at Disney,
first stepping onto a moving sidewalk
then into rows of moving chairs.
(Elderly preservationists in blue blazers load you in.)

You ride through a dimly lit tunnel.
As I said,
the dioramas are gone
so you just see recesses in the walls where they would've been.
The molded seats are wingbacks and there are tiny speakers by your ears.

And you can hear an actor (Alexander Scourby maybe?)
describing what, at the time of the fair, you presumably would've
       seen.
Eventually, though, you come back out into the light,
having basically *seen* nothing—except shadows.

Well, like I said,
I've had this dream many times.
In it, I ride because I'm in Flushing Meadows Park
and it doesn't seem like there's anything better to do.

So you give a small donation and they put you on the ride.
Who knows?
Maybe someday they'll raise enough money to replace the dioramas
but that won't be any time soon.

I wake up from this dream feeling strange
like maybe it really happened or something.
But the GM Pavilion doesn't exist anymore
and the fairgrounds are now a park.

And I haven't been back.

Pete Sussman Tells His Son about the Fair

They took me to the Fair in '64
but faded Instamatics can't convey
the brilliance of the sun—the swirl and roar,
the throngs, the marching bands—or catch the way

the summer sun flashed off the Unisphere
or how they said 2004 would be
or how we'd fly to planets far and near
or how we'd live in domes beneath the sea.

Now, looking back, it's hard to contemplate
our feelings as we wandered through the fair—
beneath the chrome cathedrals of the State.
I think we thought we saw the future there.

We couldn't get enough! We wanted more!
We were enchanted!—back in '64.

Pete Sussman Opens a Window

It was always hot in my high school and,
even in the spring,
it seemed like you could smell the blast of radiators and chalk.
And I never felt much like studying.

Geometry 1 was also my homeroom
and we had to say *under God* when we said the Pledge of Allegiance.
But, for better or worse, I never really believed much in God.

My teacher, Mrs. Steinberg, said you could see God in geometry
but I never did. And,
although I got good grades at first,
I soon fell further and further behind.
And God,
who was never there to begin with,
abandoned me even more
and I started to get *Fs*.

But I think I *did* experience God one day
when it was really hot and I was standing over by the tilt-out
    windows to get some air
because the teacher hadn't come in yet.
My hands were on the window ledge which was about waist high
when, all of a sudden, I felt something soft.
It was Jackie Feldman in a clingy mini dress,
leaning hard against the ledge so she could push open another one
    of those tilt-out windows.
To this day, I wonder whether she knew about the spiritual gift she
    was giving me.

So, for a while, at least,
Jackie Feldman convinced me that there *was* a God—
not the God of geometry but God nonetheless.

Well, ever since I completed college, I'm sure there *isn't* a God
but I still believe in Jackie Feldman
and those parts of her I'll never know again.

A Phone Call in the Dark

Sleep prevents images from occurring.
Darkness and sleep are similar.
In the darkness, in the nest of my bed,
the phone bell shatters darkness
and darkness is like the shape of your voice
which I hear in the darkness
like a letter speaking from far away.

My circadian rhythms broken,
you tell me something which I have forgotten.
Only the telling is not what informs me.
It's the sound of your voice—
not the words spoken.

If I were to walk outside, I'd see the sky,
too clear and bright to be darkness,
the moon piercing darkness like a clear beacon,
old light from stars making a new appearance on this planet.
Everywhere, I think, space is curving.

Your voice moves at the speed of light,
pulsing through me on arriving.
Stars and planets, Wallace Stevens, symbolic logic,
Will we make love again?
are the topics of discussion in the darkness
as hours sail by like long-distance minutes—
quickly and expensively making us older.

Dawn's birds sing and I fight back yawning,
the Earth's new day beginning.
The Earth, spinning on its axis toward morning,
takes me no closer to you
but keeps us turning in our thoughts
to a past not to be repeated,
keeps us turning toward darkness.

Among the Waves

In the green Gulf water
you are suspended in a perfect space
as flat light slants into late afternoon.

When I speak
a horseshoe crab sticks in my throat,
claws at my words and beliefs
as the sky is consumed by pink and orange fire.

Belief is like playing in the ocean at sunset
while the tormented sky cavorts above you
and the taste of saltwater mingles with the taste of wine on your lips.

My legs stagger under the weight of the sea.
I'm battered by the waves
and break into wreckage
long submerged under tons of water.

Looking up through layers of ocean,
I feel myself breaking and lying easy on the ocean floor
to rest there forever.

2

Pete Sussman Answers a Challenge from the Countess Lisa to Write a Sonnet in Less Than 24 Hours

"You're telling me that *you* know how to write
Elizabethan sonnets?" Lisa said.

I didn't get an ounce of sleep last night.
I dragged myself to work today half dead.

For someone whom I've never hugged or kissed,
it wasn't easy writing on command.
Though, after all, I'm such a narcissist.

But so are you!—your hair and face so planned.
That china face—the careful powder puff.

Yet, as coworkers, we can never touch.
And so I gulp down coffee, act aloof,
and focus on not liking you too much.

I watch you disappear, thin and serene—
reflected in a chromium machine.

Pete Sussman Wonders Whether He Should Write a Poem about His Zoology Teacher's Feet

I steep myself in science after work.
Anatomy is hard so I decide
to get some extra help with lizard bones
by speaking with my teacher after class.
She's young and blonde with vaguely Asian eyes
and, glancing down, I notice that her feet

are shapely in their shiny shoes. Such feet—
so little that you wonder how they work—
are startling and I have to blink. (My eyes
have dwelled on them enough.) Well, I decide
to open up to her. I tell her class
is fascinating but I make no bones

about my lack of comprehension. Bones
of reptiles don't make sense and it's a feat
identifying kingdom, phylum, class.
Forget the rest. This subject makes me work
much harder than my job. She says: "Decide
if you are serious or not." Her eyes

meet mine then dart away—those ice-blue eyes,
that upturned nose, those elevated bones.
Her lipstick glows. Abruptly, I decide
she's inaccessible. I sense defeat.
I'll never touch her stockinged feet or work
into her learnéd consciousness. Our class

will be the only time we meet. Our class
will be the only time those perfect eyes
will look at me. And, while I do my work,
I'll think of her. I'll *feel* her in my bones.
I'll write a villanelle about her feet.
Should I tell her this? I can't decide.

Our conference is over. I decide
I'm just a student in her science class.
Her breasts, her legs, her thighs, her perfect feet
are for a more deserving set of eyes.
I'm just a ragged parka over bones
who wishes he could get his brain to work.

Soon, I'll decide that I'm too old to work.
My feet will ache and death will cloud my eyes.
I'll be a set of bones in someone's class.

Pete Sussman Observes A Man Eating Out Of The Garbage

In my room, the world is beyond my understanding;
But when I walk I see that it consists of three or four hills and a cloud.

—Wallace Stevens

I'm walking through Farragut Square on a fine spring day
I've just come out of my shrink's office.
The sky's gray and it's warm.
The grass is blooming and there're beds of big red tulips all around.
People are sitting on benches.

I'm feeling uplifted because I've just had this great session
and because there are literally *scads* of hot secretaries
clicking their high heels against the pavement.

Then I notice this man eating out of the garbage.
It's warm but he's wearing a parka—
like my winter parka only three times as dirty.
His face is sunburned.
His hair and beard are matted and yellow.

The man:

>Oh, this glassy square,
these office buildings at the edge of something,
some gulf, some infinite.
And these people who float
in this gray space.

>I eat their scraps—
becoming that which has been discarded.
I live at the sleeve of their consciousness

and watch as they move from place to place without gravity.
I sleep
on pavements, on grates, suspended high above

their subterranean channels,
their tubes of transport from one emptiness to another.
They do not know who I am.
They do not understand this atmosphere,
this magnified dome,
this air that we cannot touch but always touch.

I'm a connoisseur of surfaces,
a lover of textures—this gray light
and these smells—the perfume of flowers,
the perfume of women—the glass surfaces of buildings,
light reflecting off mirrored surfaces.

I watch the seasons change.
I watch day turn to night and sometimes
to day again. I stay to one side,
out of focus, out of direct view,
wearing these spattered pants
and this my winter coat.

It's something substantial
It's as real as this hot dog
or beauty—that eternal circularity
which orients this world,
this Square.

I struggle to stand still
as the universe revolves around me.
Your contempt,
your turning away,
even the word *contempt*—

these things are far beyond me.
They lie somewhere in a region of signs

that I cannot read.
Your buildings, your societal organizations
are merely tensions, currents in the river.

Pete Sussman Leaves On A Jet Plane

You always feel fear when
your plane lifts you away
from the restrictions of the
earth. You leave with the
cabin sealed, the flight attendants
with their blank faces, their
hollow hellos, the in-flight magazine
which you're welcome to
take with you, the orange
oxygen mask that—in the
unlikely event of an emergency—
you're supposed to affix
to your own head *first*,
then to that of your
child. The plane pauses at
the runway, waiting for clearance.

In a dozen cities, you
have sat in rounded chairs
in front of observation windows.
You have stared at dull
gray carpets, stretching off into
infinity. You have lugged your
carry-on luggage down endless corridors
seeking your gate, your number.
You are nervous, afraid your
plane will come and go
without you, that your ticket
will be invalid, your flight
overbooked. You're afraid of –
a wind shear, a storm, cancellation.

Today, the ceiling is low.
The plane begins its heavy
ascent. It lumbers. It vibrates.
It is a very heavy
plane. The ground rushes past.
There is a bump—an
unevenness in the runway. Time
stretches. You are pressed back
against your seat. You twist
your head to look out
the window. The plane is
easing up. First the front
wheels, then the back
as the ground falls
away. Impossibly slowly. Pressure changes.
Ears pop. Everything is compressed.
The plane falls through an
air pocket. *This is it.* Everything
is over. The silver fuselage
will drop. It will smash
into houses, plow through buildings,
cut down cars, telephone poles.
Your body will be burnt
beyond recognition—your skin like
blackened chicken, your body parts
torn and yanked apart, spread
across a swaying field of
corn. You clutch the armrest.
Your palms sweat on to cool
vinyl. You realize the idiocy
of this action. Armrests won't
save you. Nothing will as
you fall through space and
time. Plummeting not only through
the cool gray air but
through your life. This falling
doesn't stop. It continues even

when you are safely on
the ground. Where do you
think you're going? But miraculously
the plane surges up. Up
through the cloud cover. Up
into this limitless blue dome.
You will survive this flight.
You will live a little
longer. But going from here
to there will never eliminate
your secret feeling of restraint,
your hidden fear of falling.

Without Forewarning, Sussman Quits His Job

Just let me say I've given up on words.
They don't express the things I want to say.
The feelings that are swirling through my head
aren't captured well by words like *loss* and *pain*.

Tonight, in my apartment, feeling hungry,
my lizard crawls toward me on the carpet.
(His total world's the wasteland of the carpet.)
Too bad he can't communicate in words.

Each day, I'd get to work late, feeling hungry.
Nobody asked me what I had to say.
Each day, I walked around concealing pain.
A silent storm was swirling in my head.

Things sucked so bad I fantasized I'd head
to Oregon with résumés and carpet
Multnomah Street to nullify my pain.

Just after quitting, I exchanged some words
with an administrator and I'd say
I acted pretty badly but—*look*—I was hungry
not just for recognition: I was hungry
for *clarity*. I guess I lost my head
or something snapped. I didn't want to say
You fucking bitch! but did. She shat the carpet.
However, my unnecessary words
just pissed her off; they didn't cause her pain.

My breath condenses on a window pane.
I stare out into darkness, feeling hungry
far less for recognition than soft words
like *You'll find meaning on the road ahead.*

(My lizard wanders off across the carpet.
He'll never speak or ever write an essay.)

And having quit, I don't know what I'll say
to family and friends. Will they feel pain
when, breaking in, they find me on the carpet—
confused no longer and no longer hungry—
just dead—a garbage bag around my head
and, on my chest, a Post-It without words?

Now, headache pain wells up inside my head.
My hungry lizard creeps across the carpet.
If he used words, I wonder what he'd say.

Pete Sussman Translates a Poem by Hugo von Hofmannsthal

1.

We were walking down a dirt path,
crossing the occasional wooden bridge.
Well ahead of us,
three giddy girls wearing straw bonnets were singing.
Don't you remember?

You pointed at the mountain and said,
"You know,
we should really be up there."
And—for a second—
your eyes looked—well—*strange*.

And—I don't know—
something shot through me—
like during an earthquake
when blue and white porcelain jars
ease off rough-hewn shelves

and smash on the floor
and cisterns break
and the world careens
and you have to struggle
just to stay on your feet.

For a moment, I was in two worlds—
on that cool path and also up there
at the top of the mountain.
My arm was around you
and I could feel the contour of your waist.

Somehow,
that shiver of excitement and fear
that ran through me
when I touched you for the first time
is frozen in my mind.

My arm was around you
or maybe—and I'm not sure about this—
we were flying up
over the sun washed valleys of Provence—
up over everything.

2.

This morning, sunlight moved across my face
and woke me up.
I was alone in the cottage.
As I was getting used to the idea of being awake,
I noticed a faded Italianate mural on the wall—

gods
floating up from a lush arbor. (The one outside?)
They step easily into the sky.
Weightless.
Up and up they float.

I found myself wanting to catch
the hem of one of their robes—
maybe one of the stragglers
one of the gods that—well—
let's just say was more like me than the rest

because I was remembering you
and yesterday
and our walk—
you know—
along that path.

from a translation by Paul T. Hopper

Pete Sussman Tries to Be Intentionally Clever, or "The *Fuck* Poem"

"*Pi* has to be less infinite than you."
He envied her ability to dance.
(Yard sales, for this couple, wouldn't do.)
Libido never stronger, in a trance—

lights on or off—he'd touch her pubic hair.
"I fuck better when you eat me in ad-*vaaance*—
So good," she'd sigh. He fucked her everywhere.
Dog tired then, they'd savor their romance.

"I'd eat you out more often if I could—
as no past lover ever did before."
"My hopes are high," she said. He said he would—
"'Or else.'" In turn, she fucked him like a whore.

"No, I—" he said, "I should've let you know."
Demystified, she had to let him go.

for the Duke of Orléans

Pete Sussman Receives Some Advice From His Reflection

Remember how unlovable you felt
when adolescent women shrank away?
Depressed about the hand that you'd been dealt,
you told yourself that you would have your day.

Today you seem attractive and secure
and women now delight in your caress.
You've traded constancy for the allure
of anyone who willingly wants less.

Your mop of hair is starting to turn gray.
Your jaw line, once distinct, is now less so.
Seduction has become a sad cliché.
You feel less pleasure than a year ago.

It's clear your self-esteem will not improve
until you look inside yourself for love.

After a Long Absence, the Countess Lisa Returns to Pose a Startling New Set of Interrogatories

"So you were seeing two women at once
and didn't think that one of them would leave?
Are you really that much of a dunce?
Tell me, did you honestly believe
they'd sit around and wait for you to choose
which one to wed and which to throw aside?
It sounds to me like you missed all the clues
that one—*or both*—would leave you. You denied
your own participation in events.
You saw them both yet *still* had to seduce
an endless line of sluts and innocents.
No wonder she got sick of your misuse.
And now you come to me and cry *boohoo*
because someone that you really loved left you?"

Pete Sussman—After the Storm Birds

after the storm birds
return to dark perches
the wind dies
beckoning us to return

houses ravaged we
make our way
in a long gray line
toward our village
we enter dark houses
close doors

let not the water
wash away our sins
our sins that stand apart
as this April morning
washes away our
images of ourselves

3

Pete Sussman Returns to the Musée des Beaux Arts

We do go on with our doggy lives I guess
as in some cypress trees some birds look up—
already frightened once by mighty noise,
plumes of fire, fluctuating air.

Perhaps they've heard this kind of noise before.
Perhaps they've seen other clouds of smoke.
But look—this octopus of twisted clouds,
this thing that looks like cancer in the sky.

The birds protect their chicks against the cold.
Huddling in their nests, these quiet birds
so used to sun and clouds and atmosphere
do not know what to make of this. And yet,

there they were, all smiles, jovial.
Like Icarus and his father, they were ready,
those humans in their human situation,
flying high while torturers cracked their whips.

It is a kind of love without completion,
an interrupted thing, a good idea
gone bad against the background of the blue.
The air so thin, the air so thin and clear.

The moment of the incident replays
and gradually the thing does not exist
and gradually we fall back to ourselves,
our lives, our suppers, and the nightly news.

Pete Sussman Dozes Off While Watching a Rerun of an Old *Gilligan's Island* Episode

*If not for the courage of the fearless crew,
the Minnow would be lost.*

—*Theme from* Gilligan's Island

The sky explodes and fear strikes everyone
aboard the Minnow on this three-hour tour.
We crouch in darkness, waiting for the sun.

While clouds swell up like sexy Army guns,
our tiny ship is tossed just like a whore.
The sky explodes and fear strikes everyone.

Ginger cries. Her stocking has a run.
The Skipper tries in vain to site the shore.
We crouch in darkness, waiting for the sun.

"On Maui we'd be safe," says Mary Anne
(the wholesome one) and Mr. Howell snorts.
The sky explodes and fear strikes everyone.

The smart professor tries to make a pun
and Mr. Howell's wife says "What a bore."
We crouch in darkness, waiting for the sun.

Then Gilligan looks up. A fusion sun
the color of a generator's core
explodes the sky and fear strikes everyone.
We crouch in darkness, waiting for the sun.

What Will Be Remembered

When time travel was perfected,
I took advantage of it.
Using the principles of time dilation,
I flung myself into the future.

Now, as far as I can tell,
there aren't any humans anymore.
What remains
is a desert planet with a dry sandy wind.

Flecks of lost civilizations
peer out of the sand—
a scrap of paper that says
Bill Enclosed,

cotton on a string,
something that may have been
the back of an earring,
a small blue pill.

For the most part,
buildings are gone.
The ones that remain
are little more than twisted girders,

rusting in the distance
like oil rigs rusting
under the Texas sun,
abandoned and alone.

One building that,
though crumbling,
still stands mostly intact
is the British Museum.

The roof is gone
and lies in crumbles
on the floor.
I make my way through the wreckage.

Not far from the Elgin marbles
and the Rosetta Stone
lies a room of laptops,
each on its own podium.

The signage can still be read:
Ritual Objects (Early To Mid-Twenty-First Century)
Thought To Be Used In Religious Ceremonies
Honoring The Deity Jesus Christ.

Looking up,
I see that evening is coming on.
I wait for nothing.
I feel nothing.

The Death Poem

Congratulations!
You've drawn the Death Card—
the Ace of Spades.

1.

In the morning, before work, you lie in the bathtub
and lather your body with oatmeal and honey soap.
The bathwater becomes cloudy and,
as you eye the expanse of your body partially submerged beneath it,
you imagine that the bathtub is no longer a bath
but a long satin-lined coffin
and that you are a corpse
lying in state.

2.

It can happen at any time—
this death.

You are a child in a nursery school,
playing with giant multi-colored blocks.
You've just had your morning glass of juice—
and cookies—vanilla wafers probably.
A fragrant spring breeze drifts in through an opened window.

But, unbeknownst to you,
a terrorist has planted a bomb.
It explodes
and you, most of your classmates, and your teacher
all die.

One child lives
but she is badly maimed and will not lead a normal life.

3.

This consciousness that you treasure and struggle to enrich—
this consciousness—
that takes courses,
reads books,
and sometimes learns from past errors—

this consciousness
that you have right now—
will grow dim at first,
perhaps or perhaps not,
and will stop being consciousness.
Everything—
all your experiences,
all your hopes and dreams and insights—
will be as if they never were.

In fact,
there will be no *you*
anymore.

4.

You take pills at night.
You know that if you take too many pills you will die.

The choice is yours.

5.

You are driving,
trying to remember which road you take,
which exit you get off at.
Cars stream by around you and make no sense.
You are lost.

When you finally do arrive home,
you try to remember what you went out for.

You want to play a CD
but you can't remember the name of that Italian singer—
the one who sang that song about—
about San Francisco.

Hours later, your doorbell rings.
You answer it.
A woman is standing there.
She says, "*Jeez,* I was worried sick about you."
And you look at her and try to remember her name.
She seems so familiar.
And maybe she's your daughter.
Yes, she certainly must be.

"Dad—?" she says.

6.

You are in a darkened bedroom
making love to someone you hardly know.
You are hovering at the edge of an orgasm.
You reach it and make a loud noise.
You clench your partner hard for a time
then gradually relax.
The orgasm was wonderful, you think to yourself.
Then you roll over onto your designated side of the bed and think:
No matter how many times I do this, there will always be death.

7.

A scoutmaster enters a woman's home.
She doesn't know him.
The woman's ten-year-old daughter is doing an art project on the
    kitchen table.

He tells her that he wants to talk to her mother privately and asks
    her to wait for him to finish.
He takes the mother into her bedroom and tells her he's going to
    kill her by putting a plastic bag over her head and strangling her
    until she's dead.

8.

A 56-year-old man sits on a bench at the park, reading a book.
He takes blood pressure medication but it's not working today.
At dusk, a park policeman, riding on horseback,
finds him on the ground in front of the bench—dead.
The man was never married and neither is the park policeman.

9.

Lillian feels isolated and alone.
Her boyfriend of three weeks has left her,
telling her he just can't put up with her shit.
Lillian is 43.

She cooks dinner for a close male friend and his ten-year-old
    daughter.
After dinner, she gives the child a present—
a box containing some of her favorite keepsakes.

When they're gone, she does the dishes and takes a jar of pills from
    the kitchen cabinet.
She's been saving them for just this occasion.
She undresses, puts on a nightgown, pours herself a glass of
    chardonnay, and takes the pills.
She gets into bed, swallows some more pills, and waits.

The Death Poem II

—in which Pete Sussman is elected Bishop of Rome and resolves many philosophical problems which have troubled mankind for thousands of years

1. Statements

"If you mean:
Do I believe in an old man with a gray beard up in the sky?
then, no—
but I believe there's something—
a force—that underlies everything.
Maybe God *is* the Universe
or the force behind the Universe.
It's kind of hard to express."

•

"I'm not a religious person—
I'm more *spiritual*.
My spirituality means *everything* to me."

•

"You don't believe in anything after death?
I like the Hindu idea of reincarnation.
I believe we have a purpose to fulfill
and we keep coming back till we fulfill it."

•

"I've lived before.
I'm sure of it.
I believe I was a chambermaid to Catherine of Aragon
and that I caught the eye of King Henry VIII."

2. Discussion

"When we die,
something continues—
our Essence or something."

"Is it our minds? Will we think?"

"No, we won't think.
It'll just be our essence."

"So how will it be us?"

"I don't know.
I just believe our Essence continues on after we die."

"Will each of us be separate?"

"No, I believe we'll all be part of some underlying force."

3. A Theory about a Theory

"So, the way I see it,
a lot of people believe
that when we die
our body rots
and goes into the ground.

"Meanwhile, something—

call it a Soul or an Essence
or the ineffable whatever—
lifts off of us
and goes up to some cosmic plain.

"It's like each of us
is a golden beam of light
and we feel good—real good—
because our perception of ourselves
is still there.

"And that good feeling is
like an orgasm
in outer space—
like this big continuous orgasm."

4. An Objection

"I read about a woman
who had some rare illness
where she couldn't stop orgasming.
It was extremely painful."

5. Synthesis

"Clearly, I'm not talking about a terrestrial orgasm.
This is some kind of ethereal outer space orgasm
where our Essences just feel good all the time
as they merge with each other.
There's no discomfort,
no muscle spasm or engorgement to worry about."

6. Unfortunately

Pope Pete, the Bullshit Artist of Rome,
came to me in a vision.

He said, "Wise up, Dung Beetle.
When you die, you die.
You stop being *you*.
There is no more *you*.
There's no first person *I* anymore.
Only *other* people will know that you're dead.

"Remember when you were a baby
and you fell into this world? No?
Well, you did.
You fell.

"Just as you fell into consciousness so you will fall out.
And the *value* you've placed on your life for lo these many years
will be erased as *you* will be erased."

And I told Pope Pete that I'd heard him bullshit many many times
but that I didn't believe he was bullshitting now.

And so we were one.

Pete Sussman Writes a Poem about Life

1.

There really isn't much to say about life
except that people feel they have to have interests.

Some people like baseball
while others enjoy the theater.

I was sitting at a concert earlier tonight
and a guy I happened to know was sitting on the other side of my
    wife.

I've known the guy vaguely for years and
what I know about him is that he's really "into" music.

I have my own concerns:
cosmology, consciousness, writing—

All of these things are so frail
when you think about it.

When you think about it,
most pursuits are like so much paper blowing down a street.

We get married, have children
or we stay alone or we wish we could fuck someone else.

We age. We grow feeble.
We die and are forgotten.

2.

A comet has hit the Earth and
ruined the atmosphere.

Most people die but there are still a few places—
valleys and caves perhaps—where human beings cling to life.

Civilization is gone of course
and people don't speak very much.

All they think about
is the daily struggle to find air.

Gradually,
the oxygen runs out.

The last few suffering humans gasp
their final breaths and die.

No one remembers our planet
or us.

If there are other beings out there,
they either don't notice or are too far away to care.

3.

Twenty-four leading experts were polled and the results are in:
There's no free will.

Points in time are just that—
points in time.

If you were to step off the grid
and observe time as you would the spatial dimensions,

you'd see that all points exist in a
permanent and fixed arrangement.

Quantum fluctuations only guarantee randomness—
not free will.

4.

Seize life! Seize life! I say.
Go out and live it, you asshole!

Life is a big cock!—
suck it until it explodes!

Lick life's clit till orgasms ripple through the body—
all the way into the fingers and toes!

Don't let the emptiness
expand around you after sex.

Pete Sussman Considers the Act of Remembering

1.

When I'm in the kitchen,
taking my pills and getting ready for bed,
I focus on the experience I'm having right at that moment. Then I
 think—

I'm really *not* experiencing it but *remembering* the experience.
In some sense, it's probably tomorrow already.
That's what memory is.

We remember things till we die
then we *have* no memory.
Our memories are gone, vanished.

2.

When I take Ambien and am getting ready for bed,
I observe myself remembering—trying to remember.
I'm making a conscious effort to record this moment, I tell myself.

The next day, I review my memories with my wife.
She tells me I don't remember the last half hour of being awake.
"But I do," I say. "I remember all the way up till bed time."

Then I tell her what I remember
and she tells me that I'm wrong.
"You insisted on stuff that was crazy," she says. "Acted strange.

"Do you remember you were naked on the couch
and that you'd spilled a box of Corn Pops all over yourself and the
 floor?—
You kept saying I looked like I had eight arms."

I don't remember any of that
or, now that she's brought it up,
maybe I dimly remember.

3.

When I had surgery last week, they added Versed to my IV.
"OK. We're going to start the tranquilizer now," they said.
"It'll help you relax before we put you to sleep."

When I woke up and began recounting my experiences to my
    mistress,
it was clear that I didn't remember how exactly I'd gotten into the
    operating room
or when exactly they'd shaved my abdomen.

In the O.R., they balanced a soft plastic mask lightly on my nose
    and mouth.
"We're just going to set it there, not clamp it down or anything,"
    they said.
And then there was darkness and—for a time—my brain *stopped*
    gathering memories.

"Wake up! Wake up!" they said. Time had clearly passed.
I saw three faces looking down at me.
One of them was the anesthetist who'd started my drip.

But the thing is—
I could've *not* woken up
and there'd *be* no memory.

Time wouldn't come back.
The person that I am would be gone.
and there'd be no reflecting back.

4.

When I was lying on the operating table
and they started the anesthetic and I breathed in the gas,
I went into a state from which I might *not* have returned.

But I wouldn't know because—*well*—
because there'd be no transition from sleep to death
because there'd be no more memory

and—no life going forward—
there'd be no reflecting back, no person*ness*
and my subjectivity would be gone
and then I'd never know that I was dead at all.

The Problems of Philosophy

*Thus it is our particular thoughts and feelings
that have primitive certainty.*

—*Bertrand Russell*

Something which is not the thing itself is what we touch
when we form our acquaintance with the object.

The leaf, the tree trunk (gnarled), the woman (smooth)—
her light brown hair falling over her back,

skin stretched tightly over shoulder blades—
the pen and glassine box of glistening dates—

only remarkable in the fact that these things we felt
were not the things themselves. And when

a person leaves the room forever,
we are able to retain the memories of the sense data

which were, perhaps, but not necessarily,
the indicators of some matter. What if

the external world were only a dream?
Still, we would know the data. Still,

we would have the sensations
of the woman whom we touched but only thought we touched.

A friend of mine once wrote a poem in which he said
that, at one time, sailors had such sharp vision

they could see Venus in daylight.
Today our senses have deteriorated.

It's hard to feel that my efforts to distinguish forms lead anywhere.
The leaf which curls on the palm of my hand

till the wind picks it up and knocks it away
is not the real leaf but only the indication

of something possible. So too the woman who was here but now is
    gone.
Her certainty was never assured by anything.

And when she turned around and faced me,
her white teeth and the darkness in her eyes

became stuck—like a nail—
in my particular thoughts

and I accept the existence of her *not* because I want to
but because I must.

The Chinese Room

1. The Turing Test

Place a machine in a room where nobody can see it.
Send questions in and have the machine respond.
Pay close attention to what happens.
If the answers generated by the machine are indistinguishable from
    human answers,
conclude that the machine is intelligent—
maybe even conscious.

2. The Chinese Room Argument

John Searle thought this up.

Put a guy who doesn't know Chinese in a room.
Give him a rule book.
Get a pack of index cards.
Send questions in–
slide them under the door–
in Chinese–
written in Chinese *characters*.
Instruct this dude (see below)
to follow the rules in the book.

Some sample rules:

If the character *x* comes in,
copy *y* onto an index card and send it out.

Similarly,
if character string {*x, y, z*} comes in
[for lack of better English terminology
because of course this would all be in Chinese],
send out character string {*p, q, r*}.

There are many rules of this nature
and they all follow much the same pattern.

3. *Thought Experiment*

Now,
imagine *you're* that guy—
the guy in the Chinese room.
You don't speak Chinese.
[NOTE: Even if you *do* speak Chinese in real life,
for the purposes of this exercise, imagine that you don't.]

Questions are sent in to you on index cards.
You can't read them—they're in Chinese.

But you have the rule book.

The rule book says—
blah-dee, blah-dee, blah.
You know the drill.
You read it above.

If *x*, then *y*.

The take home point here is
the rules tell you exactly which characters to copy down.

And, though there are many rules,
you're a fast reader and they're indexed well.

Dutifully, you follow the rules.
Characters come in.
You consult the rule book,
carefully copy other characters,
then send your file cards out.

The exchange of cards goes something like this:

On their index card: It's spring.
On yours: Yes, I know.
On theirs: I'm glad winter has finally come to an end.
On yours: I feel the same way.
    I thought spring would never arrive.
On theirs: Smell that jasmine!
On yours: Yes! The fragrance evokes memories of
    past springs.
On theirs: Do you remember that young virgin
    you seduced?
On yours: Quite well.
    I remember the way her skin felt–
    how she lay there–
    naked on that red blanket
    on the green lawn—
    and how it felt to glide my palms
    lightly over her nipples.

Chimes sound—
the prearranged signal that there will be no further index cards.
You're glad you don't have to copy down any more Chinese
    characters.
It was starting to become tedious.

A researcher opens the door and ushers you out of the Chinese
    room.

—How'd that feel? she asks.

—Fine, I guess.

I was worried I wasn't going to copy the Chinese characters quickly
    enough.
What was I writing?

—It's not important, she says.
Go down the hall and somebody will give you your check.
You did a good day's work.
Thank you for your time.

You regard her—
an Asian woman of perhaps 25.
Slender, pretty,
her own ethnicity unknown.
You're fairly sure she isn't Chinese.

She wears a white lab coat (open)
over a dark blouse and tight maroon miniskirt.
You note that she's wearing stockings—
and high heels.
A two-fer.

She has *beautiful* eyes,
a *dazzling* smile,
and *silky* black hair.

She extends her hand.
You take it.
The handshake is quick
and a little more firm than you're used to.

She turns and walks swiftly down the hall.

You never see her again
and you have no idea what you wrote on those cards.
You're not even sure if it was Chinese—
maybe just some random characters they made up.
You'll die without ever knowing what was on those cards.

4. The Larger Argument

Searle's right, I think. Computers can't be conscious.
They just move stuff around from place to place
according to a certain set of rules.

But if that's true, don't neurons do the same?
After all, neurons merely fire.
Surely an individual neuron can't be conscious.

So how does syntax—
an ordered set of predictable electrochemical reactions—
to a sunrise—*say*—
or to a tiny waterfall spilling over ancient rocks
deep in the woods of the Shenandoah Mountains—
the mere movement of pulses in a set order—
lead to consciousness?

And are these manipulations really any different
than the ones made by a computer
or the guy in the Chinese room?

You keep thinking you can solve it,
this problem of consciousness.
We can know everything about the brain,
know how every part is tied to every other part,
know how signals flow from place to place
but it still escapes us, lies just outside our grasp.

What gets us from syntax to *all this?*

About the Author

Herb Guggenheim was born in 1956 in Washington, DC and was raised in Silver Spring, Maryland. He received his MA from the Writing Seminars at Johns Hopkins University and his PhD from the Center for Writers at the University of Southern Mississippi. His poems and short stories have appeared in a number of literary magazines, including the *Beloit Poetry Journal*, *Gargoyle*, and the *Washington Review*. He's the author of the chapbook *Pomes, Buck Each* (1994) and the audio book *Understanding Pathological Narcissism* (2006). Visit him on the web at http://www.herbguggenheim.com. If you'd like Herb to do a reading, lecture, or workshop for your organization—or if you'd just like to give him feedback on this book—address e-mail to herb@herbguggenheim.com.